Sitting in the Shade of My Own Tree

Sitting in the Shade of My Own Tree

Poems by

Marylou Kelly Streznewski

To The Guilderland
Library,

M.K. Streznewski

Sept. 2021

Cover design by Shay Culligan

Cover photograph by Marylou Kelly Streznewski

Back Cover photograph by Thomas Streznewski

ISBN: 978-1-950462-52-0

Kelsay Books Inc.

kelsaybooks.com

502 S 1040 E, A119
American Fork, Utah 84003

For my father, William J. Kelly, who taught me to love words,
and for the members of the Christopher Bursk Spring Workshop
at the Bucks County Community College,
who have inspired me to keep trying to make the words into art.

Acknowledgments

The following poems appeared in my chapbook, *Rag Time,*
J.G.Whitthorne Press, 2002. "Sisters," "Posing," "Jello,"
"Hummingbird," and "For Lady Chatterly."

The following poems appeared in my chapbook, *Woman Words*
J.G. Whitthorne Press, 2003. "Minimum Security Facility—
Suburban," "Cancer," "Sunday Afternoon the Garden," "Song for a
Child Who Never Was," "For My Daughter, On the Changing of
Her Name," "Acorns," "Widows," "In My Daytimer," "Old
Friends," "A Crone Invades the Health Club, During a Workout,"
and "Talking on Water."

"Granddaughter's Moon" appeared in *New Millennium Writing,*
Winter, 2013.

"Marketplace" appeared in *Dying with Robert Mitchum*
Aldrich Press, 2015.

"Women Who Sit on Victorian Porches in Summer" appeared in
U.S.1, Summer Issue, Princeton, New Jersey, 2017.

Contents

Tributes

Codas

Origins

Minimum Security Facility—Suburban

It was nicely furnished.
There were no bars.
The fence, however,
was just beyond the door.

It was invisible
but strongly built
out of duty
out of love
out of fear.

I was on my honor
not to flee,
but sometimes
when all my lost music
sang across the blazing death
of an autumn afternoon,

here,
where no one watches,
I danced.

Women Who Sit on Victorian Porches in Summer

Bordentown, New Jersey, 2002

It is hot New Jersey summer. We sit,
Mother and I, with our notebooks,
listening to the tree-muffled roar
of semis groaning up the Interstate.

Up here on the bluff we see only
the far bank, a marsh misty in summer
haze despite a leaf-rippling breeze
through the shade of two ancient maples.

Out along the Delaware's edge,
Crosswicks Creek Marina shelters boats.
The once-a-day train to Camden
rattles by below us.

The traffic drones on as we write,
each in the cell of her book.
Mine is practical black, littered with clips.
Hers is a merry red plaid, a gift she says,
from someone who understands that
confusion be damned, she still writes at 95.

Antique railings in geometric iron
isolate this Victorian house
from a green strip of public park.
The gate sags open.
Gray slate slabs of the walk bump,
lurch toward the steps. Shaggy grass,
faded lawn, part weeds, bespeaks
the casual neglect of rented space.

My mother's elegant first floor includes this porch.
Tall posts, half blue, half cream create our
gray-floored gallery, improved by potted ferns
the upstairs tenant waters with great care.
Her once proud family built this mansion.
Having lived to see it sold to strangers,
she rents the room where she was born.

Sitting with us, I can see,
in their high-backed wicker chairs,
the ghosts of the Victorian women
who lived in this house: their long skirts,
piled hair, tight corsets, cotton stockings,
high button shoes. Locked into place at home,
they managed the meals, birthed the babies.
No antibiotics, not even the vote.
A life span of forty, if they were lucky.

No matter how rich,
they could not sit on this porch as we do—
in sandals and slacks, bared feet and short hair,
no hairpins to poke us, eyeglasses to clear
the blurred trees by the creek.

Only rebellious or mad could they think
the free thoughts we accept as our due;
we women who sit on Victorian porches
in summer and write what we please.

Posing

Framed by perfect blue sky, they sit for a portrait.
Three generations on the stairs to the beach house:
Mother alone on the top step, smiling her way
through her eighties, glamorous in a pink silk shirt.

The camera-wielding neighbor has an eye for symmetry.
Middle-aged sisters must be next:
one angular Bohemian with dangling earrings,
one suburban Earth Mother in baggy sweats.

Young sisters below them.
Fresh from trim careers, they show off
in sun hats and bikinis. Before

the shutter snaps—sudden as birth pangs,
she finds she cannot share this space
with any sister, cannot consent
to balance any pose. So she jokes,
jostles over the cries of the gulls until
she shatters the pose and moves
one level down because, you see
she cannot say out loud:

These belong to me.
I have paid for these sleek tanned persons:
price far beyond the Biblical groans.
I have spent my life helping babies grow
to flawed irrevocable miracles.
I have bargained with the Hag,
bartered with the Old Man and
earned the right to stand here in the sun
unbalanced,
on the third step,
my arms around my daughters.

16

Ancestry (dot) Grandmother

One sixth of me comes from
Mary Agnes Minnick Kelly.
Two generations off the boat, living
with the bigotry of *No Irish need apply,*
Ma ruled her immigrant family
with an iron hand, determined each should
succeed, Irish or not. She stares at me from
the one photo we have, stern in a long skirt,
hair in a top knot, her submissive husband
John beside her on a garden bench.

John worked for the Staten Island
Department of Sanitation,
which allows me to brag,
My Irish grandfather was a garbage man,
which Ma could not abide, and pushed,
until there was a job at the Post Office.

True or not, family legends abound.
She disowned Mae, the daughter who left nursing
to marry a man her family didn't approve,
throwing all her belongings out on the porch
that day when she came home for the last time.

There was Honora, called "Nan," required to leave
her convent when she developed TB, coming home to die.
The twins who only lived three days escaped
Ma's domineering ways.

For Willy, the son who became my father, she thought
to choose a wife, but Bessie married his brother
Frank, a New York policeman. Ma never accepted
that Little Polish Girl who became my mother.

For help in running her boarding house, she kept
Winnie and Dolly home from most of school.
Winnie never did learn to read, still saying in old age,
"I don't have my glasses, will you read this for me?"

When Dolly, the pretty one, had a child by one
of the boarders, Ma took to her bed with no visible
illness, turned her face to the wall, and died,
two years before I was born.

Teenaged Neal, the youngest, wept at the loss,
became a singer, a CPA, successes
she would have approved.

And then there was Ted. Son of a domineering woman,
he married one. On a rainy night in the depths
of the Great Depression, when he came home
one more time to say, *No work,*
his wife threw carfare at him, saying
Come back when you have a job. He never did.
Did he die in some hobo camp by a railroad track?
No one knows.

I am her namesake,
Marylou Agnes Kelly Streznewski.
"Judge not, lest you be judged," the Bible says.
The stern faced figure in the faded photo
wanted so much for her children,
will I ever understand her griefs?

The Voices of the Dead

If I listen,
I can hear my father's
playful manufactured words:
spondoolicks, and *lapsey-pals,*

my Polish grandmother call me
Dear Little-Damn-it–to-Hell,
feel her soft body warming mine
like the feather quilt in our
shared winter bed,

but all I have of Grandpa flickers
in a newsreel without sound.
To my three-year-old self he smiles
down from Olympian height,
spare, dignified and mute.

At Four I stand in the buttery sunlight
of a tall white kitchen as he
offers me homemade rock candy
from a special jar, clear glass
and twinkling.

Six looks down on a parade
from an office window
and catches her breath.
He rides a white horse
at the head of his lodge, sword
at his side, white plume of his tricorn
dipping over navy and gold braid.

Mute herself, Seven hangs back
in the corner of a shade-pulled shadowed
room where silent arms reach, reach,
too weak to hold the newborn
baby sister parents place upon
his dying bed—two months to the day
Seven frankly stares at
gray trousers, cutaway coat
rosary-wrapped hands,
the face on the satin pillow
already set in marble.

Jello

Six-year-old hands
grubby from play
wrestle the wooden spoon.
And oh! Boiling water
is so dangerous.
Carefully coached stirring:
It must all dissolve. Our
company won't like it gritty.
Vigil at refrigerated door.
Triumphal presentation.
I made it by myself.
Years,
watching soufflés rise,
saucing Tournedos Rossini
with truffles, hoping
the Peaches Melba will please,
there is that child
with awkward hands,
red jello quivering
in a clear glass bowl.

Gin and Tonic

An aluminum caddy holds eight globed
glasses trimmed with silver. They serve
well for gin and tonic. Friends admire
them, ask their source,
so Art Deco they appear.
They were purchased for their echo

of another set, forgotten, broken:
my parent's Twenties wedding gift
of glasses, a chrome cocktail shaker,
long since lost.
To cradle this rounded shape in my hand

complete with gin and tonic, evokes
a nine-year-old, a modest house on
New Year's Eve, where I in flannel robe,
wakened by my father for this turning
year, was allowed as at no other time
to hold the silver rimmed globe, drink

a tiny draught of Virginia Dare, watch
my father's smile, hear him say,
Listen for the bells, Honey,
listen for the bells.

Down the Block

Down the block was the drugstore
with the soda fountain, dark marble
Olympian source of ice cream cones.

Down the block was my eight-year-old
Odyssey, the challenge to complete
a journey in summer heat, earn
the price of a double dip—
the extra nickel my Polish Granny's
reward for making it back
before her cone could melt.

Now, like Tennyson's Odysseus
sitting on his rock, I dream
of completing my journey
before it all melts away
in fogged memory, or
my heart gives out
before the end of the block.

I Have Been a Nighthawk

For Edward Hopper

I have sat in a late night diner in Stroudsburg
with sandwiches and milk;
my father drinking coffee, staying awake.
My mother quiet, rocking my sister.

The all-night gas station in Binghamton reeked of
petroleum, the grubby bathroom smelled of urine.
I put coins in the candy machine, while my father
negotiated repairs for our faltering Ford.

On the road to the new place,
having gone broke in the old,
we passed lots of houses warm and secure,
with lights in the windows, where supper
was waiting and the bills were all paid.

My father believed with a salesman's
faith, there was always a short-cut to
things getting better.

Once in winter, we stopped on a hill facing
forked roads, hopelessly lost in moon-drenched
snow. Another disaster, it was achingly beautiful.
We sat in silence, our worries forgotten.

Daddy could always get us through.
He started the car, slid down the side
of his latest bad judgment, and found
a good road to another new town,
a furnished apartment, another new
school, my career as The New Kid,
always on my own.

Lives

Cancer

We simply don't know
they said and paid their
malpractice insurance.

We can't operate without
proper symptoms, they explained,
and the tiny bottles of drugstore
painkillers crowded the glasses off
the shelf above her kitchen sink.

When they knew, the doctors said
they were sorry. My sister replied,
I do not intend to linger, had her
red hair cut short and held court
in a sexy green nightgown
twelve hours before they came
with the knives.

Afterwards, the Philadelphia surgeon
said he was sorry too, while she
fought the sedatives, raved about
apple trees and roses, and a kindly
stranger read the Bible by her side.
She took four days to die.

In the morgue, nothing was said.
Hippocrates' brothers artfully
excised only the corneas.
They left us a flower drenched
coffin in the crematoria chapel
and a borrowed minister's word,
At the end, she was not afraid.

Sunday Afternoon: The Garden

Puttering of a small plane, circling slowly.
A hawk, huge against the sun.
Hot air on my back, purple mums nod
welcome to my sister in the garden.

To die, wrapped safe and close,
conventional funeral, conventional
headstone—part of earth, leaf, mold…

but to die and be burned and scattered—
flowers, coffin and all, scattered on the
sand, fused with wave and sky.

My sister chose that beach.
And we who live must reach for scatters,
try to capture ashes. Must we anchor
the dead in earth and boxes?

A year to the day, coming shyly across the grass,
I don't know why I bought these, my mother
brings me potted purple mums and
buries my sister in my garden.

Song for a Child Who Never Was

Nameless, sexless little might-have-been,
nature's accident both coming and going,
sent spinning into Limbo one Thursday
afternoon just before Halloween
while the living were taking their naps:

being I carried (following instructions)
in covered plastic to the hospital where
nurses ran and I lost consciousness,
they call you "a spontaneous abortion."

They use that reverberating word
to me, about you. It is the word of
black-robed justice, blind, the word of
holy-eyed men thrusting plastic bags
into politicians' faces, the word of
arm-linked women defending clinics.

In silent grieving the screamers
never think about or see, I call
the fear-faced women sisters.

But down the years,
how shall I call you?
Miscarriage?
Accident?
Foetus?
Product of conception?
Bloody pulp?
My fifth child?

602 Atlantic Avenue

Trenton, NJ

Above the grand fieldstone rancher which
now sprawls across that spacious lawn

the ghost of a converted farmhouse
sometimes rises into the sky. Inside

its green-shingled walls, there lives
a shabby second floor apartment.

A struggling violin sounds from
little sister's collapsed bedroom.

Teenagers kiss goodnight
under the ripped-out wisteria.

The family eats dinner at a kitchen
table tilted toward oblivion.

A college student studies at a card
table by the shattered front windows.

A father waits for the doctor's car
where he will die of a heart attack.

The widow spends long evenings
alone in the smashed living room.

A bride, bereft of father, poses
on the demolished front steps.

The chain saws may have finished, but
the tulip tree remains, three stories tall.

For my Daughter, Upon the Changing
of her Name

I remember forsythia,
yellow against pale green
spring sun
on the day she was born:
a morning I awoke
and was invited down the hill
to the white stucco hospital
with white linen placemats
on the trays,

to lie a whole day
watching
the birth-mover drip
into my veins,
watching
nurses listen, frown
listen
as heartbeat faltered;
going under in the tide
of gas because
they told me later,
It would be easier
if we lost her.

Special child, born with a caul.
Chinese say such persons
will be survivors
fortunate, and honored.
Twice lucky, then, the doctor says
It was wrapped around twice.
We always had a name
prepared. Too cold, it seemed

to enter in nameless welcome.
We chose plain Jane to ease
her way with the polysyllables
ancestors brought from Poland.

Palest-of-brown child,
coffee-cream belly
I caressed with such joy.
A glow somehow,
beneath the skin,
and as she grew
a look, as if to tell the world
that she had conquered
the strangling cord,
slipped into life smart enough
to use slipping to survive.

Now she has given birth
to her own new self
choosing the exotic name
I always loved, but was not
brave enough to give.

As she trained a whole new world
to call her Alexandra,
never Jane again,
I just assumed I'd be excused,
allowed to call her as I had
even before her birth; but she
corrected, still corrects me.

Stumbling and forgetting,
I call the child of the caul
and the forsythia in the sunshine—
cannot un-give what I gave,
cannot un-name
what I called forth in April.

Granddaughter's Moon

Behind us in the soft-lit house
her new mother sleeps,
her new father washes
the supper dishes.

Up to the darkened sky
I hold the fragile warmth
of six days old.
Beyond the black roof line
of a house on the next street,
the headlight of the universe
rises, inch by glowing inch.

White it is, on high beam
making luminous this deck
this neighborhood of stately trees
back fences, tomato plants,
old dogs, covered pools,
abandoned toys, a loping cat.

I want this light to fill her
wide, awakening eyes
imprint itself on her
almost blank brain, so that
having drunk silver
older than mother's milk,
on the sorrow-filled day
when she learns to cry for the moon,
she will remember, far inside,
what she already is:

Venus, goddess,
woman of the monthly power
caller of the ocean tides
priestess of the planted seed
keeper and carrier of life.

She raises her infant hand—
a reflex salutation. We are
drenched with this shining
moonlight as holy
as baptismal water.

Annie Kosko's Wooden Spoon

I

We found it when the house was sold.
It is twice as thick (twice as strong?)
as ones we find on supermarket shelves,
the handle long enough to reach the bottom
of soup kettles on the coal stove
where she cooked a hundred years ago,
stirring cabbage, boiling pierogies,
baking her own bread every day;
standing on the canvas carpet a miner's
wife had to scrub on hands and knees
in her battle with the coal dust, black,
finer than sand. Near the bowl,
the handle has carved decoration—
something we don't seem to need
for fast food preparation.

II

No one ever called her Annie!
My grandmother's name was Anna,
growls my husband,
her gray-haired grandson.

While admitting I never met her,
I can see Miss *Anna* Vargo braving
Ellis Island, her Old World packed into
the trunk that graces our front hall.

Anna is there in the serene Gibson Girl,
portrait ornately framed on
the wall of our guest room,

where I see my husband's mouth,
my oldest daughter's eyes, and only
yesterday, my granddaughter's face.

She is *Anna* again in the wedding ovals
on the wall of the den, a serious bride
whose lovely veil crumbled to cobweb
at our touch—John Kosko her groom, his
handsome face inherited by our second son.

And *Anna* I can see in the formal family
portrait. Heavy matron now, she home-birthed
eight babies, never losing one.
They treasured little Down Syndrome Pearl.
John holds her on his lap with so much love.

III

But I insist on *Annie,* despite my husband's frowns,
because I know about the tintype, the only one
I've ever seen. You have to tilt the ancient plate
to see the photo studio image of two girls:
the granny boots, long skirts and fitted jackets,
proper New York Victorian dress.

I see two best friends, the whole New World
before them, mischief in their smiles, feathers
in their hats, laughing together in the time
before she went to coal country and fell in love.
The photographer saw it.
He wrote *Annie* on the back.

The Bridesmaid's Tale

How many maids
does a bride require?
It depends on friends
who will wear
with a smile:

ruffles that jiggle
down the aisle
like a pink souffle
on the chubby one
fat curls framing
the athlete's face
for a transvestite effect

a midnight blue creation
complete with hoop,
in which one can't
sit down

skin tight ice blue satin
under which one wears nothing
that won't require joining a gym

and which one agrees to pair
with the usher who doesn't talk,
her hung over cousin, who sweats,
the married one who pinches,
his college friend, who ignores her.
It is Her day, they tell each other,
so they endure. And hide the pictures.

Widows

She holds her head up
wears long skirt and boots
stands with hand on hip
as if pride in bearing pain
before the world
could help the pain.

Widowhood is theatre of a sort,
ritual performed as if audience could
ease the loneliness
of endless dinners for one.

No audience as middle-aged
Ophelia, half-mad with grief,
inquires *How does my Lord
this many a day?*

Her shattered Hamlet stares
at his plate, ignoring
the Ghost of his murdered
dream, which sits with them,
bloody as any Banquo,
through silent suburban dinners—

so that she is the one
who sees it,
who stares it down
every day.

She holds her head up
wears long skirt and boots
stands with hand on hip
as if pride in bearing
could help the pain.

Acorns

The bride planted acorns,
a dozen in a row
across the new suburban grass.
The neighbors laughed.
The squirrels ate all but four.

One decapitation by mower
left three baby trees
looking rather foolish
out there all alone.

She planned a family but
the shy husband left her.
She spent one whole winter
staring at the fire.

She worked for causes,
fought with fools and lost,
held a job and even traveled—
middle-aged school teacher
doing Salzburg on sabbatical
because she loved the music.

In her solitude she plays Mozart.
The house is paid for.
Three oaks guard the lawn.

Observations

Lace Tablecloth

The sign said "Estate Sale."
We parked far back, walked the rutted lane
past a gray farmhouse, long neglected,
a colorful Saturday crowd of browsers,
booming auctioneer fronting the barn:

Antique lace design from the famous
Scranton Laceworks. Approximately
seventy years old. Suitable for a large table.
A few frayed stitches in one corner.
Starting bid $25.00

The cloth he held was a beautiful
swirl of ecru lace in filigree design.
We stood beside the shabby porch.
Twenty-five, I called. *Thirty,*

spoke a voice across the boards.
Thirty-five, I smiled at a farm wife
figure, stout and serious. *Forty,* she
frowned, turning toward the sagging

screen door between us, where afternoon
sunlight caught a faded housedress,
a pair of knobby, work-worn hands
in a lap, hands that twisted and twisted.

Let's go, I said, abandoning the bid
and starting toward the car.
You wanted it, said my friend.
Not that much, I replied.

Not enough to risk, every time I spread
it across my family table, the vision of
those gnarled hands, wringing,
wringing, as they auctioned off her life.

Political History

For Jackie White

Small chic Afro, dangling earrings,
round smile like a brown sun:
she has watched the Panthers
stalk her Oakland streets,
braved the smug colleagues
at a white private school,
tended her schizophrenic son,
pampered her Borzois,
rejoiced in a grandchild.

It was 1943, she tells me.
In our San Francisco block
he matched my five years exactly.
A bright-eyed Japanese boy,
my favorite playmate.

I have never forgiven them, she says,
planting the leg attached to a metal hip
which out-walks me every day.
I have never forgiven them
for taking Sami away.

Road Work

September, 2011

Traffic is stopped. They are fixing the tracks
so the New Hope and Ivyland Railroad
can follow its steam whistle on through
the woods, taking the tourists along
for a ride.

I lean out the car window, chin on my hand.
A thin line of saplings edges the road.
Bucks County corn bakes in September sun.
Orange Alert mocks the changing leaves.
A pillow of dread weights my shoulders.
Should I start stocking food, saving water?

This same angle of light, this same sun
might have shone on some far Roman
matron on Appian Way, waiting
for the chariot jam to clear. Was she
spoiled and silly, with her slaves
and her baths, her feasts and her villa,
her lush curtained cart, with no thought
of Barbarians, the end of her world?

If this is Armageddon, if this is how we end,
I would want them to know, those who dig
in our ruins, who we were, how we lived
When this road turns to rubble, all our towers
collapsed, how will they see us?

Long dead Roman lady, my slaves are electric,
preparing the feast at my villa tonight.
I don't think I am spoiled, and I do
understand that those who are coming could
shatter my world. From my comfortable cart,
here in the future, I can empathize now.

The flag woman whirls her loud orange banner.
We put chariots in gear, GO SLOW, moving on.

Marketplace

The bright song of the lace,
filigreed, seductive, sings
what the customer desires
beneath her blue burkha,
what the customer expects—
not the bomb—
not the screams
not the body parts
black, shredded—
not the song of the sirens.

A Crone Invades the Health Club During
a Workout

Daughters!

You.
In the beautiful hard bodies,
tight muscles holding
your unused wombs.
Yes, you.
In the silver spandex skin:
stop reading oracles
in your biceps and your thighs.
Divorce is not enough.

Our March is only half begun.
It will be longer than you know.
If you would lead, then you must learn
what rots, and doesn't.
which food will nourish,
which will poison children,
how to find direction
in a storm.

You.
Of the dangerous hard eyes.
You.
Whose mouth is set like weights.
Don't stare—even you
must teach
and feed
and care
and heal.

We have no Choice.
We take the children with us.
Any road we go, the boys
will grow to men, and
you will be old women
needing love.

Heed this,
or we die!

Don't push. I know
the homeless shelter
is in the next block.

Perelman Center for Advanced Medicine

Philadelphia, PA

Glass.
Glass.
Glass.
Stories and stories of daylight
draw the eyes upward in awe,
maybe a bit like going to heaven
without the clouds and the angels.

A grand staircase ascends
like a heavenly escalator
fit for the entrance of a god
and goddess, a queen and king,
or maybe Busby Berkeley—
a musical cue for leggy
half-clad chorus girls stepping
slowly down to greet us.

Glass elevators, floors suspended
on walking bridges leading to
the beehive where it matters.
The kind receptionist,
a jolly balding man,
directions down a long hall,
doctors behind locked doors,
the universal exam room where
a silent technician plants the usual
electrodes for the EKG.

He comes,
a greying, balding
white-coated man,

trailing his impressive reputation,
shakes hands, reviews why I'm here,
explains what *transeptal valve on valve*
means, spends time fast-typing papers,
while I sit mute. Only then
does he listen to my heart.
He can give me no answers
until he sees another test.
We shake hands and depart.

Back across the bridges,
down the crowded glass elevator.
Everyone is kind, making room,
letting one more on, smiling,
easing each other on the way.

A cross-section of the world, it seems,
all hoping for healing: a cancer lady
in a knitted cap, a thin young teen in
geometric tights, a wheelchair, an oxygen mask.
Black and white, tall and small, old and young,
some in fashion, but mostly the ordinary
clothes of mankind on a Tuesday in March.

We move like ants
across the vast marble floor,
glass above us,
a huge open world of space,
the healing energy of the sun.

Cell Phone Diary

Out on the terrace at concert intermission
in spite of May's evening breeze,
a gentle of moonlight, sweet air filled with blossom,
a graceful young body glowing with life,
she must call Mary Ellen, chat on her cell phone,
make plans for next Thursday—seven-thirty or eight...

Family dinner for four at the local bistro.
Daddy's home for a while. Two children
rejoice, but smiles fade to blue,
when his cell phone rings,
and Daddy gets up and walks out the door.
He stands on the sidewalk talking and nodding.
Mother stares at her plate.
Children sit quietly, listless and sad.

On the bus from New York to my Bucks County
home, a megaphone voice from the front seat
recounts what's for dinner, which soccer team
won, has her brother called Sue? As a card
carrying member of the dear human race,
am I required to care
that her pork chops have thawed?

She's a busy young mom with a van
full of kids, a left turn to make, traffic to watch.
Does she concentrate well,
both hands on the wheel?
No, she talks on her cell phone and one-hands the turn—
too busy to see that other car coming.

In My Daytimer

Unemployed clouds and blue sky
gaze down through the glass ceiling
framed by industrial geometry
to brick walls and plants.
Stacks of white concrete stairs
curve below ground.

Hot peppers in the chicken burrito
at least have potential to smack me
out of this corporate comfort.

Women wear trendy dresses.
Business suits only on the men,
one of whom leans from the stairs
to call a hearty, *Keeping you busy*
with that new contract are they?
in an *o*rganizational voice,
waves a corporate wave,
smiles a PR smile and
bounds up the stairs with
Motivational Seminar vigor.

His listener asks his table,
"How did he know we got the contract?"

A tailored solitary reads a fat novel
and reaches, sightless, for rattling potato chips.

... I like green best, and silk fabric...

... My son said her boyfriend was beating her...

Two in cropped hair and black and white dresses
lean over coffee interrupting each other.
If she writes the article...
Get the magazine more...

An iconoclast in non-designer jeans and sneakers
buries himself in the *New York Times.*

Outside, corporate trees dine on water and mulch.
A single pink-skirted secretary munches cookies
in their shade. Flowers bloom in cement
bordered beds.

If they knew, would they care,
these sitters on mesh and red leather chairs,
eating caterer's sandwiches and talking of
love and death and cantaloupe, of divorce
and how they should design the cover of
the new brochure to look like something else—
that the matron in the power suit, scribbling
importantly with her silver pen, is writing
a poem about them in her Daytimer?

Tributes

For Frida Kahlo

After a sonnet by Bernadette McBride

With well-deep dots of light, you stare back at us,
defying all our sympathies with what you believe
belongs to you, *painting your tear-dripped eyes*
in settings so bizarre we cannot reach you
in the center of your pain, your refusal
to go under, bus or no bus.

With nails, with arrows, with blood, you force
any pity away, leave us alone, to horrors
all our own. *In thorn necklace you paint yourself*
away from us, away from Rivera, but back
again to him, because, perhaps he understood,
at least from time to time.

So *paint yourself in braces,* in all the visual
realms of pain we cannot hope to feel. *Only the spirit
is left to command attention,* to make us come to terms
with what the world and pain can do to us, how
we learn by absence to appreciate what we have.
Heart, foot, mind are bound by chance, and lost,

any one, by surrender to the fear, the pain,
the ugliness we only know as surface,
subtraction from the whole, when the leg fails
to be what a leg should be, when life fails to be
what life should be. *Accident, misshapenness*
can only be a mask for what we know to be

a far greater force, far greater energy and light
no matter who is broken, who has died, who
has struggled in the night, and you expect

we will understand that broken is the tale
you wish to tell. You expect we will know
your struggle tells not only your story
but our own:

Frida of the dark eyebrows,
Frida of the flashing red skirt,
Frida, whole in your brokenness

For Janet, Found Dead in her Garden

Sail on Silver Girl, your time has come to shine.
—Paul Simon

Death is such a sneak.
Janet, watering her garden, is suddenly aware
of another presence among the flowers.

I do not think Old Death frightened her.
They had met in Hospice rooms before.
I also do not think he dared be rude, but
knew his summons, although brief,
must be as polite as to Emily for
that carriage ride.

Maybe he did offer a trip through
Doylestown's old fashioned streets,
past the houses she knew, the trees
she planted, flowers she watered,
people she nurtured. Perhaps it was
too sad to say farewell to family,
so she didn't.

These last three days I have been
followed by a voice which says,
as I look out a window at spring,
 sip my coffee, or comb my hair,
Janet will not do that anymore.

The list grows long and longer.
I read a book, pull a weed,
trim old forsythia, savor well-cold
water and try to think of where she is.

Here, inside my eyes, I see
purple tunic and silver white hair,
dainty earrings and medallion
which drew me to her in a crowd:
distinctive lady, radiating warmth.

Today I sit in the driver's seat
of my parked Blazer eating
crackers and cheese in a deserted
college parking lot while the trees,
freed by the whirling wind, fandango
in their new green. The sun warms
my lap, the sky is cornflower blue.
A good day to die, I think because,
if this really was my last day, wouldn't
I want it to be beautiful—the best trees,
the best sky, the best breeze of all?

My father's last was like this, a perfect
September Tuesday his last glimpse of sun,
an amazing grace for which I am grateful.

"Amazing Grace," how sweet the sound,
I listen to on tape, alone with my collection
of tears: Judy Collins sixties voice,
before the fog of alcohol and drugs,

some high soprano at a Peace Rally,
carrying out over a lawn where
I had just looked into the saint-shine
of Daniel Berrigan's eyes,

my actor brother-in-law's funeral
where we stood on a hilltop in the sun,
and Kira's soprano carried to the clouds,
and we all applauded because
it was, after all, his last performance.

My mother's grave, where I always knew
I would sing.

And now again, the amazing grace of Janet Hill
whose life touched mine this tiny bit—
color and light, an ear for laughter
and the play of sound—sail on Silver Girl.

Old Friends

You and me lilac,
we haven't fooled each other in years.
True, I maintain my winter distance
safe in the house, but early every Spring
I come to see what you are giving up on,
this time.

I snip little twig ends,
lean on limbs to test for rot—
limbs wrinkled to the feel
of gray paper egg cartons.
Like a vain and aging woman
disguising a threadbare coat,
you distract me with brave
outrageous blossoms
in Persian blue.

I know you see the face that
leans among your branches
going slack with age, watch as
youth slides down my cheeks,
feel the hands that wield the clippers
less sure upon your stumps,
hear this figure bend and rise
with more groans every Spring.

Year after year, old friend,
both of us feel the pinch as I indulge
in my perennial failure of nerve:
cutting off too much, too soon,
mistaking dry branches for death.

Hummingbird

A true story

At the Lincoln Memorial the President sits.
The chattering tourists in the Statuary Hall on
Capitol Hill see a tall standing man with paper
in hand. Emancipation—for whom?
Vinnie Ream made that statue.
They called her The Hummingbird.
She touched clay at sixteen, met Lincoln
at eighteen, found him, *Haunted*
by sorrow, by death and by war.
Twenty-two saw the statue
to thunderous applause.
Supporting her family, she flashed
her dark ringlets all through her twenties,
even flirted with Sherman.
She lobbied the Congress—
commission for Farragut's statue her goal.

Thirty-one, she surrendered
to a handsome lieutenant.
In the glum wedding photo
could she hear Hoxie saying,
what family legend recounts?
Live not for the world but
for love and for me. Your
work for art is ended,
these hands belong to me.

When cheers came for Farragut
she was already married.
Her life shut by duty, she entertained
generals, bore Hoxie a son.

Her salon was famous for twenty-six years.
No one shackled her mind
but her hands, her hands must have ached
for the feel of a chisel on stone.

Twenty-six years, then her heart
let her down. Wise doctors pronounced:
Suppression of feeling, from wanting to work.
Day after day, her terrified husband
begged her to live.

Hoxie bribed her to life with permission
to work. An ill fifty-seven, she started again.
In a boatswain's chair
rigged by the man that she loved,
she made two more giants
to grace the rotunda, the circle of men.

She died sculpting Sequoia,
he who carved language
for his Cherokee people.

The Nomad

For Marj Hahn

She has been a traveler, teacher, reader,
content to live out of her black Chevy Prism,
sleep on couches all across America,
see and hear what lives beneath
the desert or the subway.

She blesses the magic of New York,
loves the pigeons, wishes for a lover,
irons Barbie clothes for twin nieces,
misses them, and her twin sister.

She writes from Boulder, *I have found a home!*
Her close-cropped hair grows longer.
Her lines make a found poem:

*If everyone stopped speaking, would
this concrete at my feet become dust?
My mouth, this weary nocturnal atom,
a word takes space, so make it matter.*

*I don't like the things I'm supposed to like.
I was not impressed by Mount Rushmore.
At Grand Canyon I got the cosmic joke—
how insignificant we are in the face
of the whole universe.*

*I am a body and a spirit out there
in the world trying to reconcile
visible and invisible, hungry
for a new game.*

I'll see you in April.

Not His Mistress, and SO Not-Coy
Or
A Grad Student Walks into a Bar…

…Had we but world enough and time,
This coyness lady were no crime.
We would sit down and think which way
To walk, and pass our long love's day
Even in a university town bar
that's a really lousy pickup line.

Thou by the Indian Ganges side
Shouldst rubies find; I by the tide
Of Humber should complain.
That Ganges and Humber gig—
you could do it with a smart
phone in no time. Don't you
keep up with these things?

I would
Love you ten years before the Flood,
And you should, if you please, refuse
Till the conversion of the Jews.
Yes, we have had some awfully
wet weather, floods even, but
please, leave the Jews out.
I don't get into Israeli politics.

My vegetable love should grow
Vaster than empires, and more slow
'You a vegan or something?
Let me get this straight:
there is now vegetarian sex?'

An hundred years should go to praise
Thine eyes, and on thy forehead gaze;
Two hundred to adore each breast,
But thirty thousand to the rest;
An age at least to every part,
And the last age should show your heart.
For, lady you deserve this state,
Nor would I love at lower rate.
All this ages loving this and that;
I thought you were in a hurry.

But at my back I always hear
Time's winged chariot hurrying near;
I get it—you're having some of that
winged chariot mid-life crisis thing.
I thought you looked familiar. You
are that older guy who teaches
Seventeenth Century Lit. It is time
you faced it Sir, you are over.

Coeds don't dig the gray hair
and tweeds any more. 'Stopped
sitting up front and gazing at you,
have they? Look, it's like this:
nobody wants a father figure
these days. It's the age of Justin Bieber,
man. Get yourself some jeans and
let your hair grow over your eyes.'

And yonder all before us lie
Deserts of vast eternity.
All that deserts and vast eternity stuff
is for old people. We are young, and...

Thy beauty shall no more be found,
Nor, in thy marble vault shall sound
My echoing song; then worms shall try
Thy long preserved virginity
worms in my—eeyoo, that's gross!

And your quaint honor turn to dust,
And into ashes all my lust:
The grave's a fine and private place,
But none, I think, do there embrace.
Getting it on in a coffin is cool now.
Obviously, you haven't seen Twilight.

Now therefore, while the youthful hue
Sits on thy skin like morning dew,
And while thy willing soul transpires
At every pore with instant fires,
I am perspiring; it's warm in here.

Now let us sport us while we may,
And now, like amorous birds of prey
Rather at once our time devour,
Than languish in his slow-chapped power.
Let us roll all our strength and
Our sweetness up into one ball,
And tear our pleasures with rough strife
Through the iron gates of life
Birds of prey, tearing open iron gates—
this is getting creepy. 'You into S&M?'

Thus, though we cannot make our sun
Stand still, yet we will make him run.
Oh you literary types are all alike!
Hemingway wanted the earth to move.
You want to stop the sun. Thanks
for the beer Dude, but I'm the one
who has to run.

For Lady Chatterly

Funny, it wasn't knowing in her bones
the grunt work of pushing an invalid's
chair up a hill that did it. Her own cripple
had forbidden himself wheels. He sat
grumbling, methodically tying himself
to his own chair.

Not even her three-year nun's bed
whose twisted sheets bespoke not
lover's struggles, but the tangled dreams
of sleeping strangers.

No, it arrived during a spring rain,
as she changed her clothes by the window
after work—this wayward desire to
roll naked, over and over
in the cold wet grass.

The Duchess Has Her Say

*For Lucrezia deMedici: Married at 14 to the Duke of Ferrara,
dead at 17, under "suspicious circumstances."*
             —Inspiration for Robert Browning's poem.

That's my last Duchess.
Always, he begins with that,
bringing all his visitors here.
Drawing back the curtain
reveals, in one dramatic flourish,
both my beauty and his power.

Looking as though she were alive,
reminding the Count's messenger
what could happen to one who
does not appreciate the Duke's
proposal for his daughter's hand.
I mention Fra Pandolf by design.
Even artists bow to his will—
or pretend that they do.

He speaks of my white mule,
my truest friend once I was sold
by marriage into this house.
The gardener was ordered to kill
poor Pepito. I was made to watch,
to teach me to respect
A nine-hundred-years-old name.
Was that title such a burden
on his less-than-manly frame?

My generous ways enraged him,
but they became my shield.
He believes he *gave commands,*
stopping all the smiles together.
The poisoned drink he ordered

never crossed my lips, because
I too had power—my commands
obeyed by those who loved me.

Fra Pandolf brought a gentle sleeping
potion concealed among his paints.
My father sent it—out of guilt I think,
writing, *Should the need arise.*
We burned his note.

My brave maid Maria exchanged
the vials. No writhing struggle;
I slept peacefully away.
Dear servant, she risked her life
to make the puzzled Duke believe
she knew an ancient art, and
smoothed my face to spare him pain.

Poor little Countess, will he bring her
here, I wonder, as soon as she arrives,
draw the curtain with his usual flourish,
tell her, *That's my last Duchess?*
Fra Pandolf has promised to paint
the Count's fair daughter's self,
and honor her as he honored me.

*   *   *   *

Now, each evening as the shadows gather
around him, the grand Duke of Ferrara
roars at his servants, *Stop that clip-clop noise!*
I will kill the one who makes it!
Pepito and I still enjoy riding along the terrace,
especially at twilight.

Codas

Talking on Water

The same questions every day.
The answers drown, sucked down
into a sea of confusion, swirling
away with the name of her
favorite niece, the word for napkin,
what she had for breakfast, how
many times she has worn
the same blue shirt.
"I don't remember," is her mantra.

Failing eyes engender fears.
Our endless reassurance swims away
on a sea of fuzzy faces, dulled colors,
twilight on a sunny day.
She no longer mentions
how much she misses her books.

Most days she is happy being cared for,
grateful for showers, polished nails,
hot coffee and doughnuts, amused at
a granddaughter's gift of red satin pajamas.

As I watch her napping quietly
under an afghan she designed
when she could still see, she
sails away behind closed eyes,
her face already like the mask
which waits not far from here.

I think of Ophelia, drifting
on the water, singing.

Cooking Spaghetti

Blue enamel pot filled with boiling water,
vapor escaping through the shiny exhaust
fan, sits ready for cooking spaghetti.

Standing at my elbow, my sister offers,
If you put them in like pick-up sticks
the strands won't stick together. So I do,

remembering the fourteen-year-old who
tried to keep house while others worked
to keep us going, producing fused spaghetti

and regular scolding. *You'd never know*
we grew up in the same kitchen, I reply,
and we laugh together.

Even now I am grateful for help.
I make jackstraws of pasta each time
I cook it, hear her voice, her laugh,
though she's thirty years dead.

The Mirror Talks Back

The face God sees, that men perhaps, see too.
—Borges

Lying down only makes you look
face-lifted, not younger.
Straight on, you can get away with a lot.
Tilt chin up to ease age and wrinkles.
Smile. A nice improvement.
Change the lighting. Lower
makes you glow, you know.
Makeup never hurts, especially
lipstick—Revlon Red, and eyebrows.

Bring this mirror's twin, the hand-held
second opinion, to see what others see,
even maybe God or your Guardian Angel,
if she is watching.

Who is this lady anyway? You never
see her from this other point of view:
her whole face hatched with wrinkles,
saggy neck, and oh, the hair, all disarranged.
My gosh one ear sticks out .
She almost has a bald spot,
the hairdresser calls her double cowlick,
combs it over.

At thirty, you really liked this face,
said to it one morning, yes, that's
the face I wanted all along. Now they say
you look more like your mother every day.
She made it to over one hundred, looking fine.
Good luck.

A Summoning Spell For the Death of my Mother

She was called Yadviga, Yaja, Hedwig, Hattie

Owl, mare, moon, stones
Owl, mare, moon, stones
Owl, mare, moon, stones
     Mountain, River of Heaven
     Four-legs keep watch:

Boat,
  bring guides for the journey.
  Those who passed over, come,
  gather at Hedwig's bed:

Husband,
lead the way with your jaunty walk.
Daughter,
smile to make her feel at home.
Son-in-law
take Hattie's arm, toss your black hair

Sister,
greet Yadviga with joy.
Mother, call gently,
"Yaja, come through the door."

Door, open brightly Light, shine softly,
arms, let go, hands, unfold
     legs, be still, head rest, rest
        eyes, close in peace.
        Room, stay quiet.
        The boat is waiting.
Let her go, let her go.
  Four-legs keep watch.
     Under the moon,
     owl wings fold.

My Ghosts Are Not

wraiths in draperies trailing
across the lawn in midnight mist
        or
spirits playing poltergeist games
tipping bookcases, smashing china
        or
pookahs screeching on the stairs
howling in the chimney
        or
"A man who looks like Grandpa,"
the five-year-old claims she saw.

Mostly, they remain well-behaved,
doing their haunting quietly:

the earrings she wore to my wedding
the park where he played with me as a child.

Sisters

We have known
the small peace while food cooks
over a fire, standing and thinking,
staring out over whatever lies
beyond the window.

We have known
the twist of fingers squeezing moisture:
wringing a cloth, wiping a counter,
washing a child, cleaning off blood.

We have known
the feel of dirt in a garden
potting plants, crumbled in fingers
in a field, in a graveyard.

We have known
the inner wrist of silk against the cheek
an urgent lover, a suckling child
quiet at dawn.

We have known
eyes demanding from their depths
that we heal, that we understand,
that we submit.

We have known
clothes, light and dark,
draping us in pleasure
binding us in servitude
as we are daughters, mothers,
brides, widows—
as we are sisters.

About the Author

Marylou Kelly Streznewski's career has included theater, journalism, and the teaching of writing on high school, college and community levels. As a member of the International Women's Writing Guild, she has served as a workshop director at their annual summer conferences. Her short fiction and poetry have appeared in national publications, and two chapbooks, *Rag Time* and *Woman Words*, are housed in the chapbook collection of Poet's House (NYC). A third chapbook, *Dying with Robert Mitchum,* has been published by Aldrich Press. She has received the Muse Award from the Bucks County Community College for "contributions to poetry in Bucks County."

Her first non-fiction book, *Gifted Grownups: The Mixed Blessing of Extraordinary Potential,* a study of one hundred gifted adults (John Wiley & Sons) appears in libraries worldwide, as a textbook in graduate courses, and has been translated into Chinese and published in Taiwan. It is currently under arrangement to be published in Dutch in the Netherlands. Most recently, Streznewski's second non-fiction book is *Heart Rending—Heart Mending: Saved by Medical Science, Healed by Ancient Wisdom,* a research-based memoir depicting, in both prose and poetry, her survival of massive open heart surgery using integrative medicine modalities (J.G. Whitthorne Press). Holder of a Master's degree from The College of New Jersey, Streznewski lives on a Bucks County Pennsylvania acre with her husband Tom.